PROFESSOR CHOCOLATE PRESENTS:

NEW YORK CITY'S
Hot Cocoa
ACTIVITY GUIDE

BY **ROB MONAHAN** AND **NEILL ALLEVA**

COPYRIGHT

We Own This Book, Please Enjoy It

Copyright © 2012 by Neill Alleva and Rob Monahan.
All Rights Reserved.

All tour names and maps in this guide are reserved and trademarked by Chocological Publishing. Professor Chocolate™ is a trademark of Neill Alleva and Rob Monahan.

First Published by
Chocological Publishing
73-31 71st Street
Glendale, NY 11385

Printed by Lightning Source
ISBN 978-0-9844580-2-8
First Edition
2 4 6 8 10 9 7 5 3 1

ORDERING INFORMATION

Discounts are available on purchases of ten (10) or more books. We offer special discounts, buying options, and consignment deals to chocolate shops, bookstores, corporations, associations, and others. For details, please contact the publisher at :

professors@professorchocolate.com

PUBLISHER'S NOTE:

Please note that we have made every effort to ensure accuracy of all information contained herein at the time of publication. It is always best to check that information is still up to date before beginning any chocolate-finding mission. If any incorrect information is found, please contact Rob and Neill at professorchocolate@mac.com at your earliest convenience and we will gladly modify the text.

The authors, editors, and publisher cannot be held responsible for the experiences of readers while tasting and touring. Your safety is important to us. Stay alert and aware of your surroundings at all time.

Descriptions of the shops and products in this guide are based on the observations of the authors. No remuneration of any kind was exchanged for any profile included in this guide.

THE ISLAND OF Manhattan AND SURROUNDING AREAS

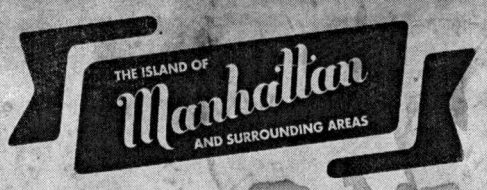

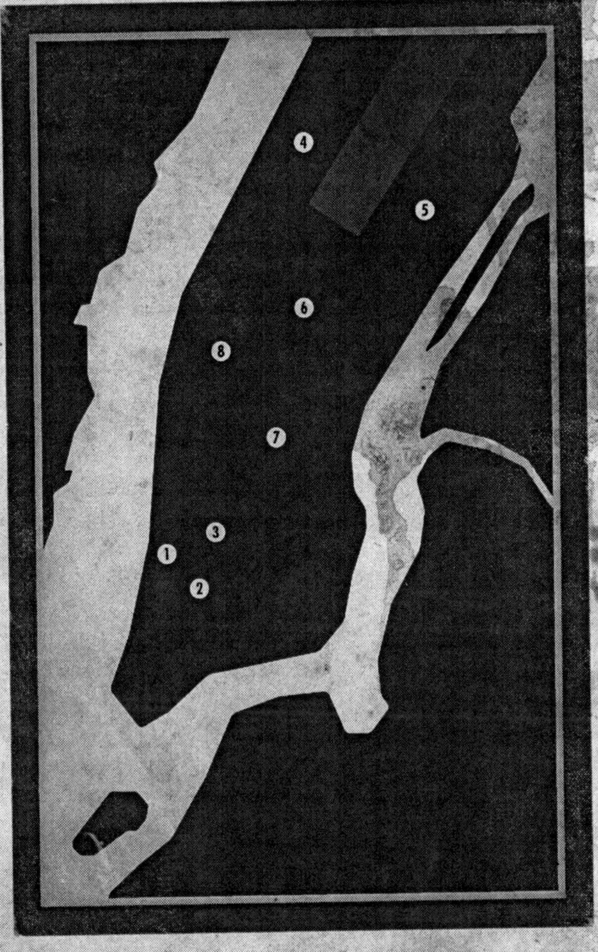

COLOPHON

This Book Brought to You by the Following Chocophiles

The Professors quite obviously love chocolate, but we love trees more. Environmental protection is among some of our top priorities. We use a printer that has received Chain of Custody (CoC) certifications from the following: The Forest Stewardship Council™ (FSC™), Programme for the Endorsement of Forest Certification™ (PEFC™), and The Sustainable Forestry Initiative® (SFI®).

Chain of Custody (CoC) is an accounting system that tracks wood fiber through the different stages of production: from the forest, to the mill, to the paper, to the printer and ultimately to the finished book. For publishers, and ultimately consumers, CoC ensures the integrity of the paper supply chain and that the paper used in printed books come from responsibly-managed forests.

In creating this book, we have made every effort to include the full spectrum of palate-provoking 'mouthfeels' represented by the Magnitude of Chocolate Density scale as created by Niko Triantafillou from dessertbuzz.com. This book is not meant to list the 16 best cups of hot chocolate/hot cocoa in NYC. It is meant to be the start of the process. Namely, the process by which an individual may determine their own perfect cup, and then share their findings with others.

Future editions of this book will include a completely new set of cocoa-creator masterpieces. It should be noted that the Professors use the terms hot cocoa, hot chocolate and drinking chocolate interchangeably at the expense of accuracy, and for the sake of simplicity and user friendliness. After all, one woman's mud is another woman's water. Who are we to judge?

This book and its cover were designed by Kurt Jeske. He can be reached via email at kurtjeske@me.com and more of his work can be viewed at bykurtjeske.com. This book contains the following fonts: 'Buttermilk' by Jessica Hische, 'Egyptienne' by Adrian Fruitiger, and 'Futura' by Paul Renner.

INTRODUCTION

We Love Chocolate, How 'Bout You?

The tasty secret of the cacao (kah-KOW) tree and the story of how chocolate grew from a local Mesoamerican beverage into a global sweet encompasses many cultures and continents.

It was the famous Carl von Linne, widely known as Linnaeus, whose binomial system of naming and classifying gave the "chocolate tree" its scientific name. The naming of such has remained unchanged since 1753. Being somewhat fond of chocolate, Linnaeus concocted the first name, *Theobroma*, meaning "food of the gods," inspired from the Greeks. The second name in the classification, *cacao*, stems from an even more complex linguistic history.

The Olmec, a group of people living in what is today the coast of the Gulf of Mexico, most likely were the first to domesticate *Theobroma cacao*. Data is slightly on the scarce side, but linguist have surmised that the word cacao, was not only used by the Olmecs around 1000 BC, but was also passed on to the likes of the mighty Mayans. By 400 AD, the Maya were drinking chocolate out of small vessel pots. The secrets of how to process the cacao beans into a drink were improved upon and thus again forwarded; this time to the Aztecs. It was the Aztecs who named the chocolate beverage xocolatl, literally meaning "bitter drink."

The Aztecs attributed the creation of the cacao plant to their god Quetzalcoatl who, descended from heaven on a beam of a morning star carrying a cacao tree stolen from paradise.

Though the final product, xocolatl, was quaffed in large quantities by the likes of Montezuma, the chocolate drink did not touch the lips of average folk. It was a delicacy and would remain so for quite some time. The beans themselves however, were used monetarily by most residing in Mesoamerica. Columbus, having encountered both the bean and the drink, remarked how the natives of the land scurried to pick-up scattered cacao beans, treating them like pieces of gold. It wasn't until over one hundred years after the Spanish conquest that the bean was shipped to Spain for consumption.

Once the Cacao bean did reach the shores of Europe, it was still produced in the form of a drink, but this time, ingredients such as honey and vanilla were added to make it more palatable for the European tongue. The drinking of chocolate continued from its Aztec roots as a product for the wealthy, being much too expensive for the common person. Chocolate was sipped at fancy dinner parties and among royalty, some even choosing to drink it out of a gold cup.

AN INCREDIBLY BRIEF
AND SELECTIVE
HISTORY OF
HOT CHOCOLATE.

1) An ancient drink called 'chocolatl' was made from roasted cocoa beans, water and a little spice.

2) The Olmecs, the oldest civilization of the Americas (1500-400 BC), were most likely the first consumers and traders of cacao, followed by the Mayans, who consumed cacao-based drinks.

3) Montezuma, emperor of Mexico (1466–1520) drank his 'chocolatl' cold, in a golden goblet.

4) Montezuma drank his 'chocolatl' before entering his harem, believing that it possessed aphrodisiac qualities.

5) By the mid 17th century, the Spanish mixed in sugar with their fashionable chocolate drink.

6) Chocolate drinking became 'hot' amongst the masses (mid-17th century) soon after the Spanish court used chocolate as a dowry when marrying into other European courts.

7) By the early 18th century, coffee houses in Paris and London began serving drinking chocolate. Soon, they became 'chocolate houses.'

8) Many years later, 'chocolate houses' became a term for gentlemen's clubs.

9) Thomas Jefferson was quite fond of chocolate, amongst other luxuries.

10) The ancient Mexican-Indian word, chocolatl comes stems from a blend of the terms <u>choco</u>, meaning 'foam' and <u>atl</u> meaning 'water.'

☕ TABLE OF

Professor Chocolate's Hot Cocoa Activity Guide

① ☆ ② ☆ ③ ☆ ④ ☆

D'town West
Pgs. 7–13

SoHo
Pgs. 17–23

NoHo
Pgs. 27–33

U.W.S.
Pgs. 37–43

FRANÇOIS PAYARD & JACQUES TORRES
▼

VOSGES & MARIE BELLE
▼

OTTO & MAX BRENNER
▼

GROM & SHAKE SHACK
▼

i.

Preference — Preference — Preference — Preference

ii.

Preference — Preference

iii.

Preference

☆ *this book also contains eight bespoke cocoa recipes by authorities in the field*

♥ **Visit each pair of shops and, based on your findings,** ♥

CONTENTS

Find Your Favorite New York Cup of Sweetness

⑤ U.E.S.
Pgs. 47–53

ALICE'S TEA CUP & LADY M CAKES

⑥ Midtown
Pgs. 57–63

BROUCHON BAKERY & MICHEL CLUIZEL

⑦ Flatiron
Pgs. 67–73

L.A. BURDICK & CITY BAKERY

⑧ Chelsea
Pgs. 77–83

THREE TARTS & CAFÉ GRUMPY

i. Preference | Preference | Preference | Preference

ii. Preference | Preference

iii. Preference

(it's always wise to re-visit all for full certainty...)

The Favorite

❤ compare and determine who has your favorite cocoa! ❤

Match-Up One
Downtown West

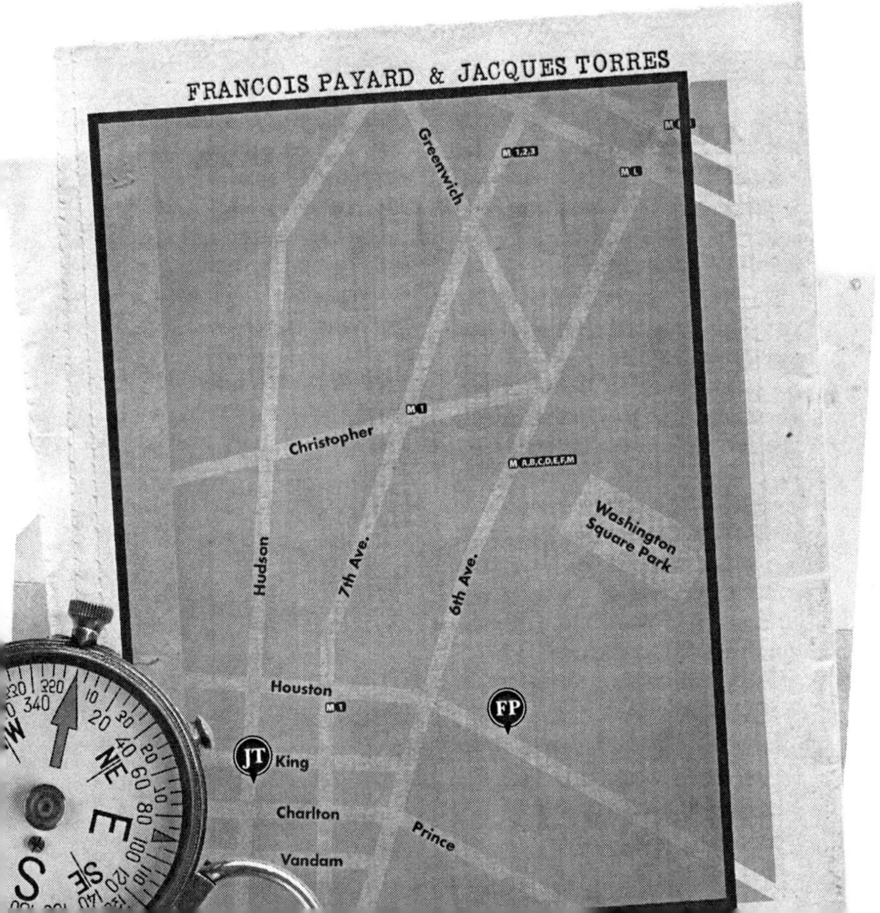

FRANCOIS PAYARD & JACQUES TORRES

Downtown West

FRANCOIS PAYARD

116 West Houston Street
New York, NY 10012
212.995.0888
fpbnyc.com

MON – THURS: 7AM – 8PM .... FRI & SAT: 7AM–10PM .... SUN: 9AM – 8PM

🍺 CLASSIC

François Payard Bakery is nestled between two of Manhattan's shopper and eater-friendly neighborhoods, SoHo and the West Village. Payard's French-inspired locale makes for a nifty spot not only for chocolate, but yummy snacks as well.

The heavy foot-trafficked niche yields to passersby, much like ourselves, in the mood for a milky and smooth blend of hot chocolate. The portions of which are perfect for savoring on a long mid-winter's stroll. If strollin' the streets isn't your cup of tea, there is plenty of room to sit and catch a glimpse of the mini chocolate factory. Striking a conversation with one of Payard's well-trained employees is in fact more likely to happen than not, always warm and gracious.

The affable Payard is well-known for his French pastries, which are certainly a treat any day of the week. Quite shockingly, however, we decided to pair our hot chocolate not with a sweet pastry but with the savory prosciutto and ricotta sandwich! Sound tasty to you? Believe us when we say that the savory cheese and meat blissfully melted in our mouths when we washed it down with a sip of hot chocolate.

NIBBIT François Payard is good friends with the masterful French chef, Jacques Pépin.

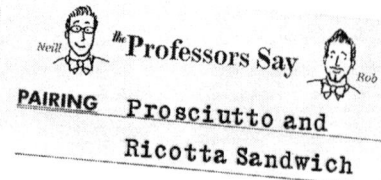

Match-Up One

JACQUES TORRES

350 Hudson Street
New York, NY 10014
212.414.2462
mrchocolate.com

MON – SAT: 9AM – 7PM .... SUN: 10AM – 6PM

🍫 CLASSIC & "WICKED"

The name Jacques Torres in New York City is as synonymous with chocolate as Cheerios are to breakfast. Torres' chocolate conjures up images of a Willy Wonka-like figure happily crafting all kinds of chocolate goodies.

If you're lucky, you may just catch Torres at his Chocolate Haven location, stirring, sampling, and ambling around his chocolate factory. Torres and company take hot chocolate so seriously that there is a counter purely dedicated to the noble endeavor of crafting a hot chocolate that some rate as the best of the best. Do not be deceived by the small portions, they are rich and full of winter-time warmth, personally made for you.

You will not see the barista pull out a jug of sludgy hot chocolate mix, just pure goodness for you and your tummy. Try with a marshmallow for a complete chocolate submersion. Make no mistake, this is "big" hot chocolate. Meaning the smooth and silky texture is purely derived from the hand-crafted nature of this very special concoction.

Think about it, the chocolate used to create this delectable little dream is roasted, tempered, and solidified just a few feet away. Talk about fresh. For those livin' on the wild side, try Jacques' "Wicked" Hot Chocolate, made with ground cinnamon and sweet ancho chili peppers.

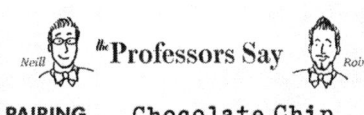

PAIRING   Chocolate Chip Cookie

Downtown West

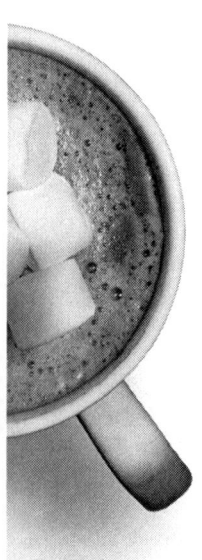

PAYARD — iced cocoa

PAYARD — François

Match-Up One

TORRES – P.C. visits

TORRES – the Classic

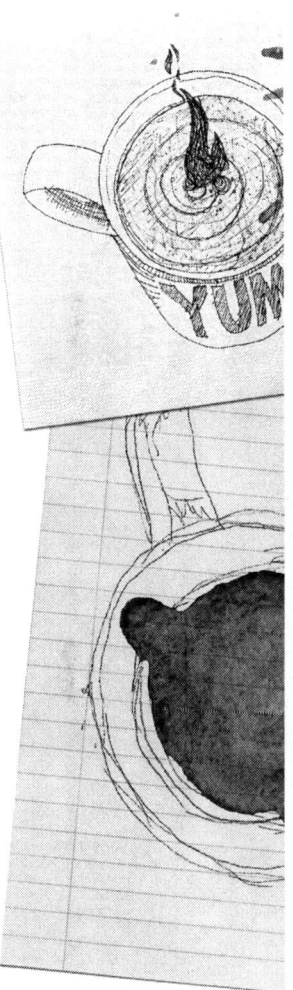

Downtown West

FRANÇOIS PAYARD

NO. 7

NAME / NOM *Downtown West*

FLAVOR .... ☆☆☆☆☆

TEXTURE .... ☆☆☆☆☆

PRESENTATION .... ☆☆☆☆☆

VALUE .... ☆☆☆☆☆

♥ Share it with us online at ♥

Match-Up One

JACQUES TORRES

FLAVOR............ ☆☆☆☆☆

TEXTURE........... ☆☆☆☆☆

PRESENTATION....... ☆☆☆☆☆

VALUE.............. ☆☆☆☆☆

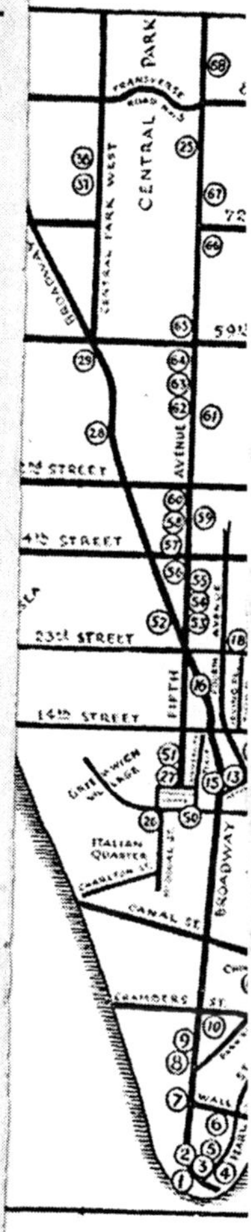

_____
_____
_____
_____
_____
_____
_____
_____
_____
_____
_____

www.ProfessorChocolate.com

Bespoke Cocoa

NIBMOR

Heather K. Terry and Jennifer Love met while attending the Institute for Integrative Nutrition in 2009. They became fast friends and when Heather started making chocolate with no refined sugar out of her kitchen, Jennifer saw a great business opportunity. Together they created Nibmor so that people could 'nibble more,' not feel guilty about their choice and reach their health and wellness goals. All NibMor products are 100% USDA Organic, with no refined sugar. They are all Vegan, Kosher, Gluten-Free, Dairy Free and Non-GMO. Quite simply—the way it should be. Not only are these products healthy, they are amazingly delicious too! Jennifer and Heather travel the world to find you the healthiest most sustainable, tasty treats on the market.

nibmor.com

Recipe No. 1

Pumpkin Pie Hot Chocolate

- 8 oz Almond Milk (or whatever your 'milk' preference is)
- 2 HEAPING tablespoons NibMor 6-Spice Drinking Chocolate
- 2-1/2 tablespoons pumpkin puree

Using a sauce pan, start to heat the 'milk' over a medium heat. Add in the Drinking Chocolate mix and pumpkin puree. Use a whisk to mix it well and break down the puree. Do not boil but heat long enough to see steam coming off the top. Serve in mugs—Enjoy!

Match-Up Two

SoHo

VOSGES & MARIE BELLE

SoHo

VOSGES

132 Spring Street
New York, NY 10012
212.625.2929
vosgeschocolate.com

MON – SUN: 11AM – 8PM

🍫 AZTEC, PARiSIENNE, AND BIANCA

Ah Vosges...The Professors do not specifically frequent this location because they have a crush on founder, Katrina Markoff (Ed: we really do). We go because you can find an eclectic, and always delicious selection ranging from toffee to chocolate and bacon pancakes—a personal favorite of ours.

The purple-hued SoHo shop is brimming with a chic sense of style, almost like you're entering a clothing boutique. Every taste here is an experience. Most exciting about winter visits to Vosges is that your hot chocolate is served in a tall, yet elegant shot glass.

For something different, we slowly sipped the zippy Aztec Hot Chocolate- with ancho and chipotle chillies, Ceylon cinnamon, Madagascar vanilla and cornmeal.

Can't handle the heat? The Parisienne and Bianca are both equally tasty and slightly more delicate hot chocolates. The Parisienne is Madagascar vanilla and dark chocolate; the Bianca an Australian lemon myrtle and lavender flower and vanilla powder and white chocolate. Whichever you choose, just know that to us, all three are good for the soul.

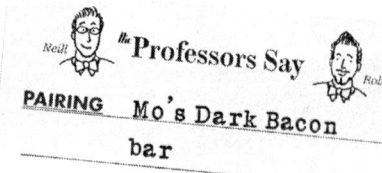

The Professors Say

PAIRING Mo's Dark Bacon bar

Match-Up Two

MARIE BELLE

484 Broome Street
New York, NY 10012
212.925.6999
mariebelle.com

MON – SUN: 11AM – 7PM

🍵 PANELLA, AZTEC, DARK, SPICY, MOCHA, MAYA, WHITE, MILK HAZELNUT

It wasn't very long ago that Marie Belle was selling its edible-art confections at the corner of Prince and Mott in SoHo. It was their Aztec hot chocolate (which the Professors each have a canister of at home) that made them a well-deserved recipient of the "Oprah bump."

Lines started stretching around the corner and the rest is history. Nowadays, we are lucky enough to enjoy close to a dozen different types of hot and cold chocolate drinks in their shop/café on Broome Street.

If you're lucky, you may catch a glimpse of Maribel Lieberman or her charming and ever well-dressed nephew Rodolfo. He runs the shop and many of the day-to-day operations. When visiting in the Summer, be sure to have the iced cardamom…one of our all-time favorites!

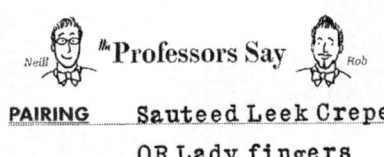

The Professors Say

PAIRING	Sauteed Leek Crepe
	OR Lady fingers

SoHo

VOSGES — exotic indeed

VOSGES — interior,
filled with delights

Match-Up Two

M.B. — P.C. visits

M.B. — the Aztec

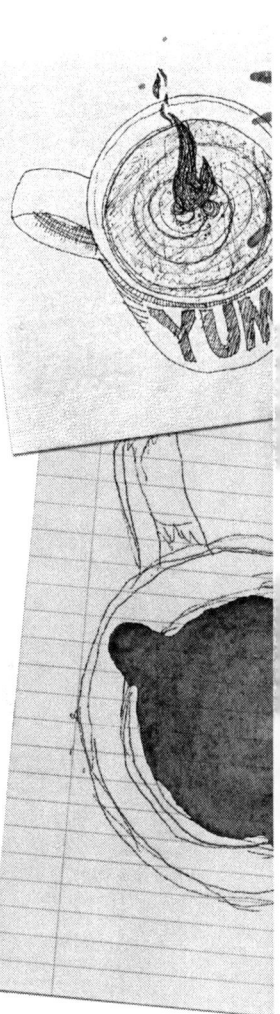

SoHo

VOSGES

FLAVOR .... ☆☆☆☆☆

TEXTURE .... ☆☆☆☆☆

PRESENTATION .... ☆☆☆☆☆

VALUE .... ☆☆☆☆☆

Match-Up Two

MARIE BELLE

FLAVOR.................. ☆☆☆☆☆

TEXTURE................ ☆☆☆☆☆

PRESENTATION........ ☆☆☆☆☆

VALUE.................... ☆☆☆☆☆

_____
_____
_____
_____
_____
_____
_____
_____
_____
_____
_____
_____

♥ www.ProfessorChocolate.com ♥

2 CHICKS

How 2 Chicks hatched…What do you do when life hands you lemons? Toss em' aside and pick up a crock-pot of chocolate. That's what Elyissia's mom did when a car accident put a wrench in her plans. So she did what any other self-respecting chick from Queens would do and started her own kick-ass chocolate business. Elyissia stayed close to the nest and followed in her mom's powerful footsteps, and 2 Chicks with Chocolate was officially born.

Check them out online at 2chickswithchocolate.com

"Fire"

Microwave or boil 1/2 cup of milk & 1/2 cup of cream...

Whisk in 1/3 cup (2oz) of 2 Chicks Fire and Ice™ Mix...

Portion into cups and serve IMMEDIATELY—serves 2...

Enjoy!

Match-Up Three

NoHo

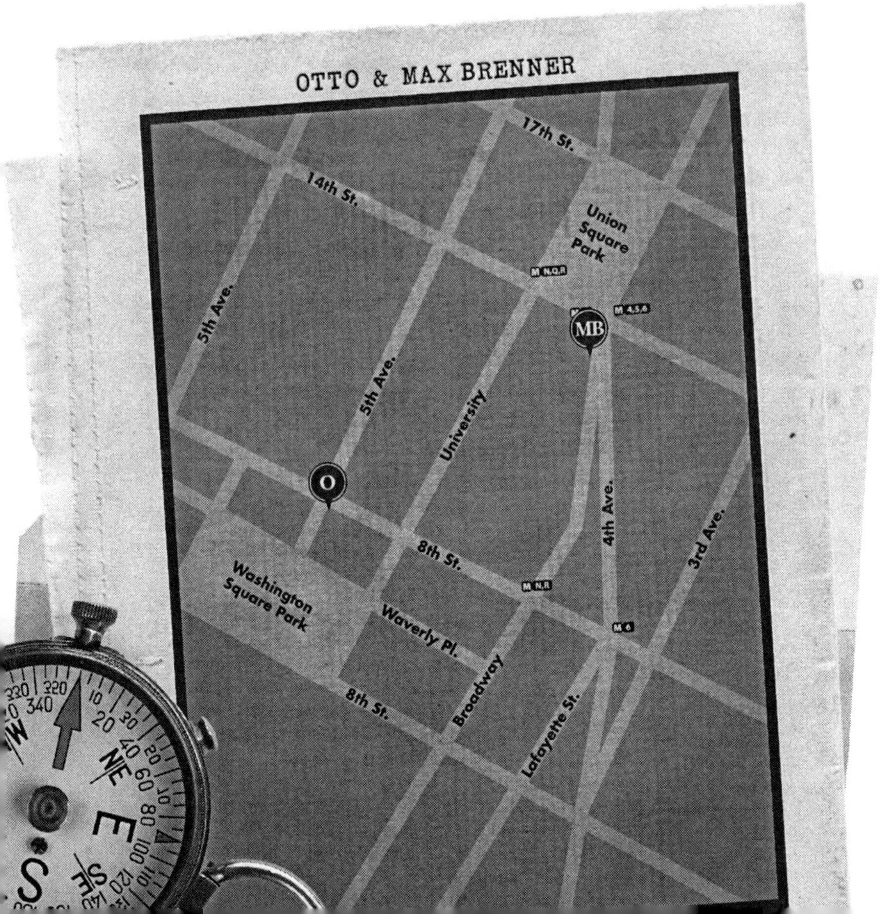

NoHo

OTTO

1 Fifth Avenue
New York, NY 10003
212.995.9559
ottopizzeria.com

MON – SUN: 11.30AM – 12AM

🍫 DARK HAZELNUT

These days you just can't meander too far off the grid without bumping into at least one of Mario Batali's luscious creations. Enter Otto, just north of Washington Square Park.

The warm and vibrant restaurant is best known for its pizza and salads, but the hand-crafted, Italian-inspired hot chocolate is worth its weight in gold. Served in a fashionable cup, with a dainty cookie on the side. The hot chocolate's sexy name, gianduja calda, is so earned by the addition of the crushed hazelnuts, an Italian tradition. The velvet majesty of this hot chocolate is best quaffed after you've indulged in your pizza/carb-overload. Go with friends and go frequently – Batali is known to chat it up with his loyal set of customers.

NIBBIT For an additional taste of classically-crafted hazelnut chocolate, visit Eataly in the Flatiron District.

the **Professors Say** *Neill* / *Rob*

<u>PAIRING</u>   Quattro Formaggio Pizza

Match-Up Three

MAX BRENNER

841 Broadway
New York, NY 10003
646.467.8803
maxbrenner.com

MON–THURS: 9AM–12AM .... FRI–SAT: 9AM–2AM .... SUN: 9AM–11PM

🍫 DARK, MILK, WHITE, ITALIAN THICK, MEXICAN SPICY, SWISS WHIPPED

Who is Max Brenner you ask? Well, no one can dispute that "he" is a pioneer in the chocolate industry. The company name is actually a combination of Max Fichtman and Oded Brenner, who launched the business together in Israel.

Eventually Fichtman bowed out, leaving Oded, "The Bald Man," to take on the persona of Max Brenner. Prepare yourself for a Wonka-esque experience like no other. You can't say we didn't warn you.

Once you navigate through the throngs of choco-crazy consumers, you can find a seat and start perusing through the half-inch thick menu filled with chocolate madness! There are simply too many different types of chocolate drinks to mention here but we'd be remiss if we didn't mention one that we particularly love...the Dark Suckao.

Mmmmmm.

NIBBIT If you're feeling adventurous (you should be), try the black and tan beer-battered Vidalia rings with dark chocolate ranch dressing.

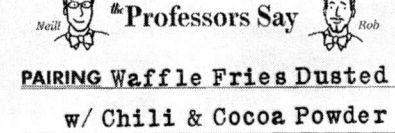

the Professors Say

PAIRING Waffle Fries Dusted w/ Chili & Cocoa Powder

NoHo

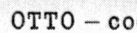

OTTO — cocoa superstar

OTTO — gotta have a pizza too!

Match-Up Three

BRENNER — P.C. visits

BRENNER — D.I.Y. cocoa experience...amazing

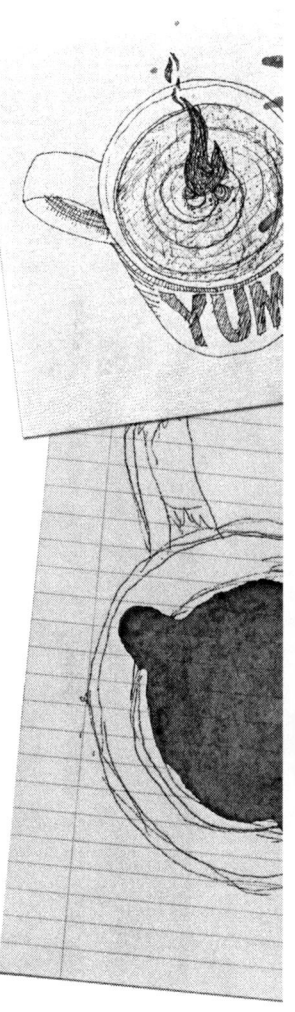

OTTO

FLAVOR .... ☆☆☆☆☆

TEXTURE .... ☆☆☆☆☆

PRESENTATION .... ☆☆☆☆☆

VALUE .... ☆☆☆☆☆

Share it with us online at

Match-Up Three

MAX BRENNER

FLAVOR............ ☆☆☆☆☆

TEXTURE........... ☆☆☆☆☆

PRESENTATION...... ☆☆☆☆☆

VALUE............. ☆☆☆☆☆

www.ProfessorChocolate.com

Bespoke Cocoa

ILENE C. SHANE

Ralph Lauren's longtime personal chef Ilene, creates chocolate indulgences so rich and delicious they will lead to moments of ecstasy. Ilene creatively uses her nostalgia for classic confections and re-invents them using high-quality Belgian chocolate. With well-developed instincts for flavor, she takes old-time, handmade favorite ingredients such as peanut butter, marshmallow and caramel to craft sumptuous chocolates that are both familiar and completely original.

Through many conversations with her friend and soon-to-be business partner, Iris Libby, SweetBliss was born. Iris had the courage and business savvy, and Ilene had the love of food and talent to bring flavors together. On February 7, 2002, they launched the line of vintage, gourmet chocolates SweetBliss is now famous for.

See her work online at sweetbliss.com

Recipe No. 3

Recipe

A Simple Reward

- Prepared Hot Chocolate/Coffee
- Kaplunks by Ilene Shane

Step 1, Prepare your favorite unflavored hot cocoa, drinking chocolate or coffee

Step 2, Enrich your hot chocolate or favorite drink by adding a <u>SweetBliss Kaplunk</u>. Each dark Belgian chocolate Kaplunk shell is filled with flavored handmade marshmallow. Get a mixture of the following flavors in each package : Vanilla Marshmallow, Habanero Cinnamon Marshmallow, Mint Marshmallow and Banana Marshmallow.

Step 3, Enjoy!!

Match-Up Four
Upper West Side

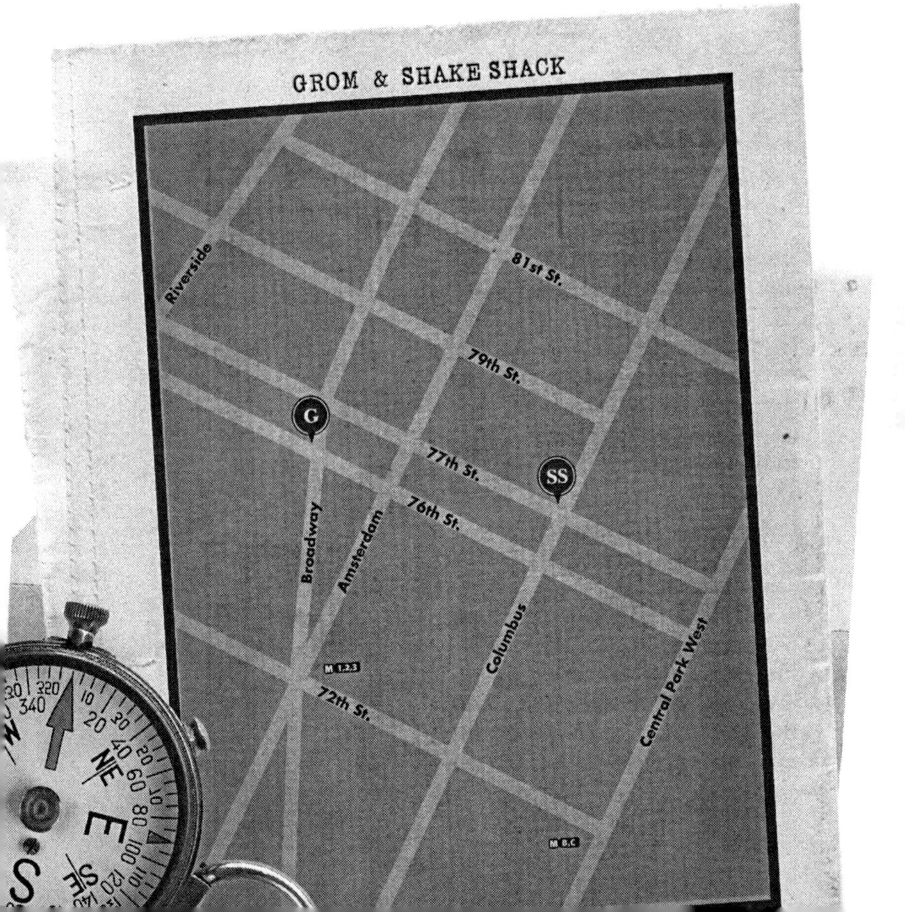

GROM & SHAKE SHACK

GROM

2165 Broadway
New York, NY 10024
(212) 362-1837
grom.it/eng

MON – SUN: 12PM – 11PM

🍨 AFFOGOTO (OVER GELATO), DARK, MILK, BACIO

Two Piedmontese and a cow walk into a bar...have you heard this one? Neither have we. That's because Federico Grom and Guido Martinetti, the company's founders, and the gelato that they produce are (seriously) NO JOKE! Not only are they committed to growing, finding and using the best ingredients that agriculture has to offer, they also try exceedingly hard to do it in the greenest way possible.

This Italian duo now have stores throughout the homeland as well as Paris, Tokyo, and of course our beloved NYC. Also noteworthy is the fact that they have complete allergen information for everything on their menu. The care for the customer and the environment, coupled with extremely high standards of production and presentation makes Grom one of our favorite stops, no matter what city we are in.

We leave you with these words of wisdom: "When in New York, do as the Piedmontese do... have some affogato con gelato."

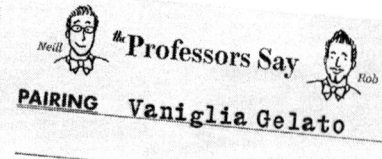

PAIRING Vaniglia Gelato

Match-Up Four

SHAKE SHACK

366 Columbus Avenue
New York, NY 10024
646.747.8770
shakeshack.com

MON – SUN: 10¾AM – 11PM

🍫 MALTED HOT CHOCOLATE *(CHANGES SEASONALLY)*

Believe it or not, Danny Meyers' Shake Shack offers one of the creamiest and most comforting hot chocolates on this planet (as if the burgers weren't good enough!). Salted Peanut Butter, Classic, and now Malted Hot Chocolate are some of the seasonal choices. The price is also VERY reasonable compared to some of the overpriced competition we have tried.

Shake Shack's multiple locations are very busy during the weekend, so look for the "C-Line." (The "B-Line" is usually inundated with burger-mongers, hungry for their fix). The cravenly delicious Salted Peanut Butter Hot Chocolate is perfection in a cup, a reflection of everything that is Shake Shack. Meyer's emphasis on hospitality and perfection can literally be sipped and tasted in any one of these artfully-crafted concoctions.

The Professors have attended some of his public speaking engagements and have enjoyed his company almost as much as you will enjoy your next cup at one of his locations.

NIBBIT Try adding some gluten-free frozen custard with marshmallow topping ON TOP of your cocoa for some real insanity.

the Professors Say

PAIRING   Double
           Shack Burger

U.W.S.

GROM — a beautiful thing

Our Hot Chocolate: real chocolate

Our Hot Chocolate is made the traditional Italian way, using the best chocolate from single high quality cultivations in Latin America, fresh milk and white cane sugar without any preservatives or artificial additives. Warm up your winter with our densely flavored hot chocolate!

GROM — real!

Match-Up Four

SHAKE SHACK — Professor Approved

SHACK SHACK — burgers are also amazing!

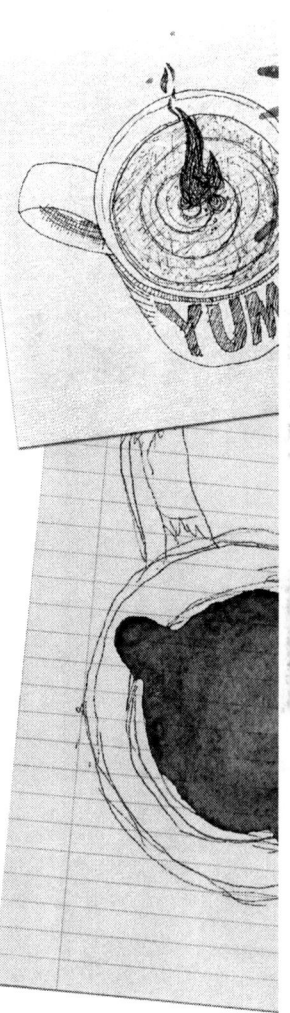

U.W.S.

NAME / NOM: Upper West Side
NO. 4

GROM

FLAVOR .... ☆☆☆☆☆

TEXTURE .... ☆☆☆☆☆

PRESENTATION .... ☆☆☆☆☆

VALUE .... ☆☆☆☆☆

♥ Share it with us online at ♥

Match-Up Four

SHAKE SHACK

FLAVOR.................... ☆☆☆☆☆

TEXTURE.................. ☆☆☆☆☆

PRESENTATION........ ☆☆☆☆☆

VALUE...................... ☆☆☆☆☆

SANDRA HAKIM

Sandra's story is a classic American tale of inspiration and entrepreneurialism. Born in Baghdad, Iraq, Sandra and her family immigrated to the Detroit suburbs when she was 14. Even as a child, Sandra had an aesthetic gift, winning awards for her drawing and painting. That passion, and a love of working with people, drove her to spend nearly a decade in the film and fashion industry as a makeup artist.

Throughout her career, Sandra took every opportunity to travel the world, sampling local flavors along the way. Her love of food ultimately drove Sandra to a major career transition which repurposed her artistic skills: culinary school. At the Natural Gourmet Institute, Sandra learned the technical skills she needed to launch her career in the culinary arts, and also discovered a passion for pastry and confections. She further honed this specialty by studying European pastry and chocolate in Switzerland, the cradle of elite sweets! After winning academic accolades for her chocolate work, Sandra returned to New York and set up an independent chocolate operation while working for some of the biggest names in the New York artisanal chocolate world.

These experiences equipped Sandra with an understanding of the entire chocolate production process, from bean to bar. As a life-long chocolate lover from a family of chocoholics, Sandra is excited to bring European techniques and global flavors to the United States.

–Visit Sandra at BaseemaChocolate.com

Recipe No. 4

Baseema Chocolate

Makes 4 medium cups
— 200g 52% Dark Coverture,
  (I use Felchlin)
— 1/4 Cup Cream
— 2 Cups of water
— 4 Table Spoons of Nido milk powder
— Pinch of Maldon sea salt

Heat water and cream together and bring to a simmer. Remove from heat. Add the chocolate and mix with electric hand blender for one minute, then add the powered milk and sea salt. Mix again until everything has dissolved. Next, bring the mixture back to the heat for one minute, simmer and serve.

Secret — You can always add a Tonka bean to the cream and water. Remove it before adding the chocolate. I love the taste and fragrance it gives. Enjoy!

Match-Up Five

Upper East Side

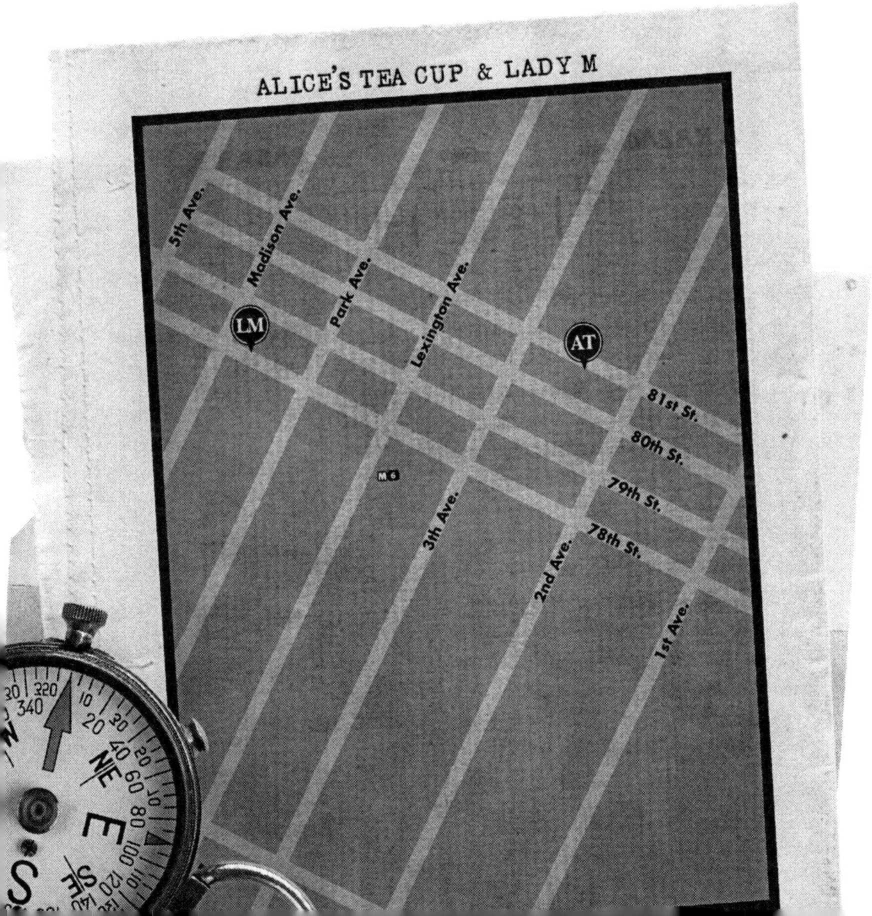

ALICE'S TEA CUP & LADY M

U.E.S.

ALICE'S TEA CUP 3

220 E. 81st Street
New York, NY 10028
212.734.4TEA (4832)
alicesteacup.com

MON – SUN: 8AM – 8PM

☕ CLASSIC, LOCO COCO, ROOIBOS-INFUSED

Charles Lutwidge Dodgson, eat your heart out…(and drink your tea)! Us Professors have been amiably referred to as "curiouser and curiouser," our works even being placed in the literary nonsense category. With that in mind, we truly appreciate the philosophy and vision of the Fox sisters in creating Alice's Tea Cup.

Their shops have taken the art of drinking tea and returned it to what it once was (and still is) in certain parts of the world… an experience. We have been to three different locations and have never been disappointed.

There's nothing quite like sitting on either side of a tower of scones and jam while sipping some fantastic hot cocoa. We chose this particular location for this book strictly based on geography, but we'd go down the rabbit hole any day and anywhere to enjoy the afternoon delights we have found here.

Major props to Haley and Lauren Fox for creating the sumptuous Rooibos-infused hot cocoa; and to all of you who are reading this… "Lapsang Souchong to all, and to all a good night."

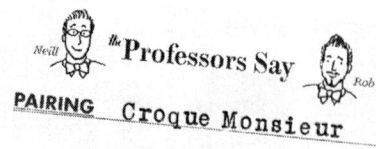

the Professors Say

PAIRING Croque Monsieur

Match-Up Five

LADY M CONFECTIONS

41 E. 78th St.
New York, NY 10075
212.452.2222
ladymconfections.com

MON – FRI: 10AM – 7PM .... SAT: 11AM – 7PM .... SUN: 11AM – 6PM

🍫 DARK BELGIAN

Where in the world is Ken Romaniszyn? We aren't exactly sure but we'd like to personally thank him for his amazing French-inspired meets Japanese-flavored masterpieces.

We would be risking serious insult if we referred to them simply as "cakes," though technically that is what these picture-perfect pastries really are. These pristine confections can be found adorning the tables of Manhattan's swankiest restaurants, the list of private clientele is nothing to sneeze at either.

To experience the decadent hot chocolate, you will need to proceed to the Cake Boutique on the Upper East Side. The setting there is beyond pristine, with a clean, white, minimalist décor and an attractive presentation, staff, and seating area. While you are there, scratch and sniff to uncover the mystery of who "Lady M" really is...

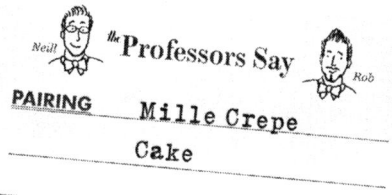

PAIRING Mille Crepe Cake

U.E.S.

ALICE'S – P.C. visits

ALICE'S – Excitement

Match-Up Five

LADY M — Simple and sweet

LADY M — Mmmmm...cake

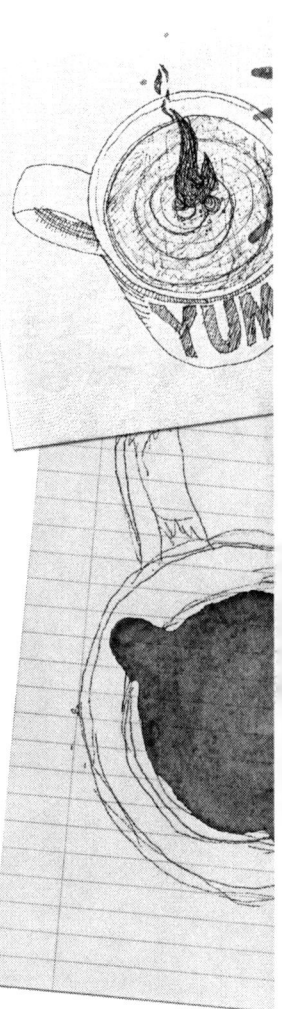

ALICE'S TEA CUP

FLAVOR.................... ☆☆☆☆☆

TEXTURE................... ☆☆☆☆☆

PRESENTATION......... ☆☆☆☆☆

VALUE...................... ☆☆☆☆☆

NAME / NOM: Upper East Side
NO. 5

Match-Up Five

LADY M CAKES

FLAVOR............ ☆☆☆☆☆

TEXTURE........... ☆☆☆☆☆

PRESENTATION....... ☆☆☆☆☆

VALUE.............. ☆☆☆☆☆

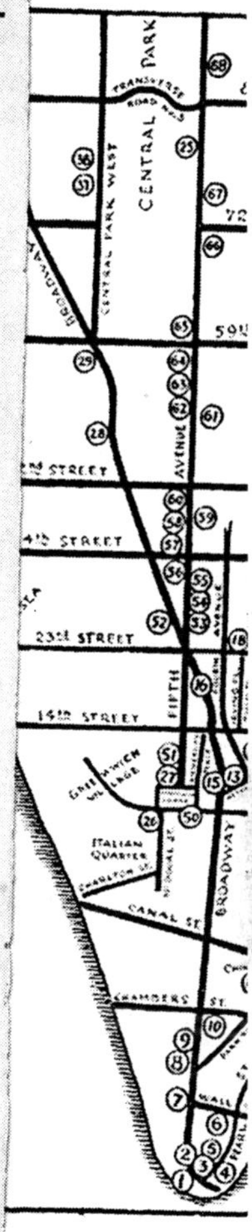

_____
_____
_____
_____
_____
_____
_____
_____
_____
_____
_____

♥ www.ProfessorChocolate.com ♥

Bespoke Cocoa

LUCKY CHOCOLATES

"All my life I've liked making things. If a life is like a tapestry then most lives have at least one strong central thread that creates the pattern. In my tapestry, it's creativity. My brain gets an idea, and then I'm actually hard put to stop it from becoming reality. I love to create whole worlds, ambiance, food, mood, everything. It's a mixed blessing. And that's how I got here…I wanted to make healthy chocolates, chocolates with interesting flavor profiles, and with depth and strong tastes. I wanted to make tiny, pretty, condensed, intense pieces of art. Art which people would consume so I could make more. I found sources, organic & fair trade chocolate, organic sugar, agave syrup. I learned the chemistry…how to temper chocolate and how to work with it. I found it was a complex subject with a lot of content. It was something I could really get my teeth into. I wanted to learn all I could and started experimenting. I started Lucky Chocolates or really, it became Lucky's. I hope Lucky's will continue for a long time—I still have lots of ideas."

-Rae Stang

Luckychocolates.com

LUCKY'S HOT LIQUID TRUFFLE

Serves 2

- 4oz 70% chocolate chopped into bits
- 4oz heavy cream, heated to 120F
- dash vanilla
- pinch good salt like Malden

Mix chocolate into hot cream whisk cream and chocolate together or use steam wand of espresso machine until it's very thick & glossy. Spoon into espresso cups & top with fresh whipped cream.

variations: top whipped cream with pinch chili powder, cinnamon or candy cane chips

Match-Up Six

Midtown

BOUCHON BAKERY & MICHEL CLUIZEL

Midtown

BOUCHON BAKERY

One Rockefeller Center
New York, NY 10020
212.782.3890
bouchonbakery.com

MON – FRI: 7AM – 7PM .... SAT – SUN: 8AM –8PM

ORIGINAL *(HOUSEMADE CHOCOLATE SYRUP, CINNAMON, MILK)*

Anyone who teaches Adam Sandler to make "the world's greatest sandwich" and also consults for the movie Ratatouille, probably knows a thing or two about cooking.

Luckily for us, Thomas Keller also knows quite a bit about running a great business and bringing us some of NYC's most-prized baked goods. Working in kitchens on the east coast during his teenage summers allowed Keller to be discovered and trained by a renowned French-born master chef.

He has been honing his craft and winning prestigious culinary awards ever since. Bouchon Bakery not only has some of our favorite macarons (no, not macaroons) in the city, but an elegant and insatiable hot chocolate as well. With locations in the AOL/Time Warner building and in Rockefeller Plaza, Bouchon Bakery has as much trouble getting noticed as Anthony Bourdain would have at a vegan festival.

With the quality of food and drink that he serves, Keller has no trouble keeping us coming back for more, and more, and more.

Keller's hyper-attention to detail and orgasmic ingredients keeps us coming back ad infinitum.

PAIRING Macarons

Match-Up Six

MICHEL CLUIZEL

584 5th Avenue
New York, NY 10036
646.415.9126
chocolatmichelcluizel.com

MON – FRI: 8½AM – 7PM .... SAT: 11AM – 7PM .... SUN: 12PM – 6PM

🍫 MILK, WHITE, DARK, AND HAZELNUT

The vast tourist throngs along 5th Avenue can be intimidating for a tourist and frustrating for a native. Fear not. French chocolate import, Michel Cluizel, offers a much needed francophile respite.

Cluizel's cozy chocolate café showcases the best of French bon bons and truffles. Though shipped from France, Cluizel has been known to visit his beloved Manhattan shop.

Hot Chocolate is anything but an afterthought, many folks stroll in here just for their hot chocolate blends of dark, milk, or white. There is also the option of one of two types: Drinking Chocolate and Classic Hot Chocolate (the Drinking Chocolate has a much thicker consistency).

The dark, milk, and white cocoa beans are scooped from a canister where they have been soaked in vanilla bourbon. Unable to deny ourselves anything chocolate and soaked in bourbon, we indulge ourselves with all three and take time to share.

This hot chocolate threesome is so luscious and satisfying, we find no reason to bother pairing it with any food. This hot chocolate, like Cluizel on 5th Ave, can stand on its own.

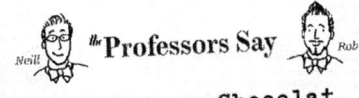

PAIRING   Pain au Chocolat

Midtown

BOUCHON – possibilities

BOUCHON – P.C. visits

Match-Up Six

CLUIZEL — P.C. visits

CLUIZEL — milk chocolate

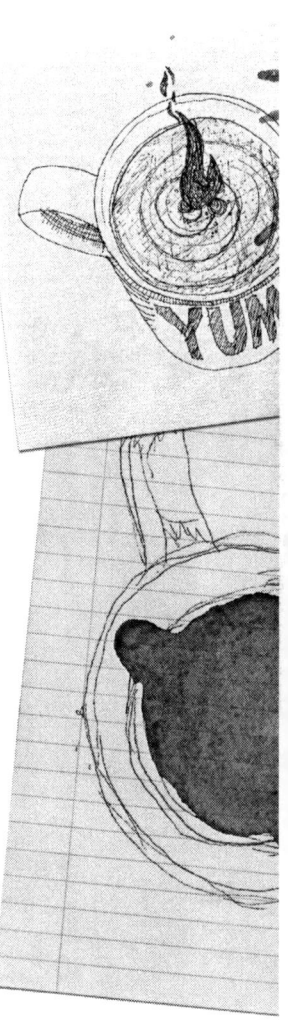

Midtown

NO. 6

NAME / NOM: Midtown

BROUCHON BAKERY

FLAVOR .... ☆☆☆☆☆

TEXTURE .... ☆☆☆☆☆

PRESENTATION .... ☆☆☆☆☆

VALUE .... ☆☆☆☆☆

♥ Share it with us online at ♥

Match-Up Six

MICHEL CLUIZEL

FLAVOR .... ☆ ☆ ☆ ☆ ☆

TEXTURE .... ☆ ☆ ☆ ☆ ☆

PRESENTATION .... ☆ ☆ ☆ ☆ ☆

VALUE .... ☆ ☆ ☆ ☆ ☆

_____
_____
_____
_____
_____
_____
_____
_____
_____
_____
_____
_____
_____

www.ProfessorChocolate.com

Bespoke Cocoa

18TH CENTURY DRINKING CHOCOLATE

During the 18th and 19th centuries, London and other European cities were crawling with coffee and chocolate houses, much like our modern cafés. The recipe below is for a decadent, yet simple version of hot chocolate that has been around since 1700.

This will make two cups of drinking chocolate, authentic as it gets, but be sure to use a high quality 75% to 80% chocolate bar. Following this method of making hot chocolate will yield a creamier and smoother chocolate concoction. Note: This hot chocolate recipe is meant to be done slowly and with patience, very much unlike grocery store hot cocoa mix that gets heated in the microwave.

RECIPE

2 cups of whole milk
1 high quality chocolate bar, chopped into bits
2 tablespoons of water
1 ounce of brown sugar
2 saucepans
1 glass bowl

Add a few inches of water into one of the saucepans, placing a heat-proof glass bowl on top, but do not let it touch the water. Place the chopped chocolate into the glass bowl along with 2 tablespoons of water. Melt the chocolate gently in the water, mother it a little by stirring.

In the second saucepan, add the milk and bring to a boil, then stir in the brown sugar. Once sugar has dissolved into milk, the milk is again boiling, and the chocolate is melted in the glass bowl, slowly stir the milk into the chocolate—a little at a time. Keep the first saucepan to simmer and stir while milk is gently being poured into the glass bowl. Pour into your chalice and enjoy!

Match-Up Seven

Flatiron

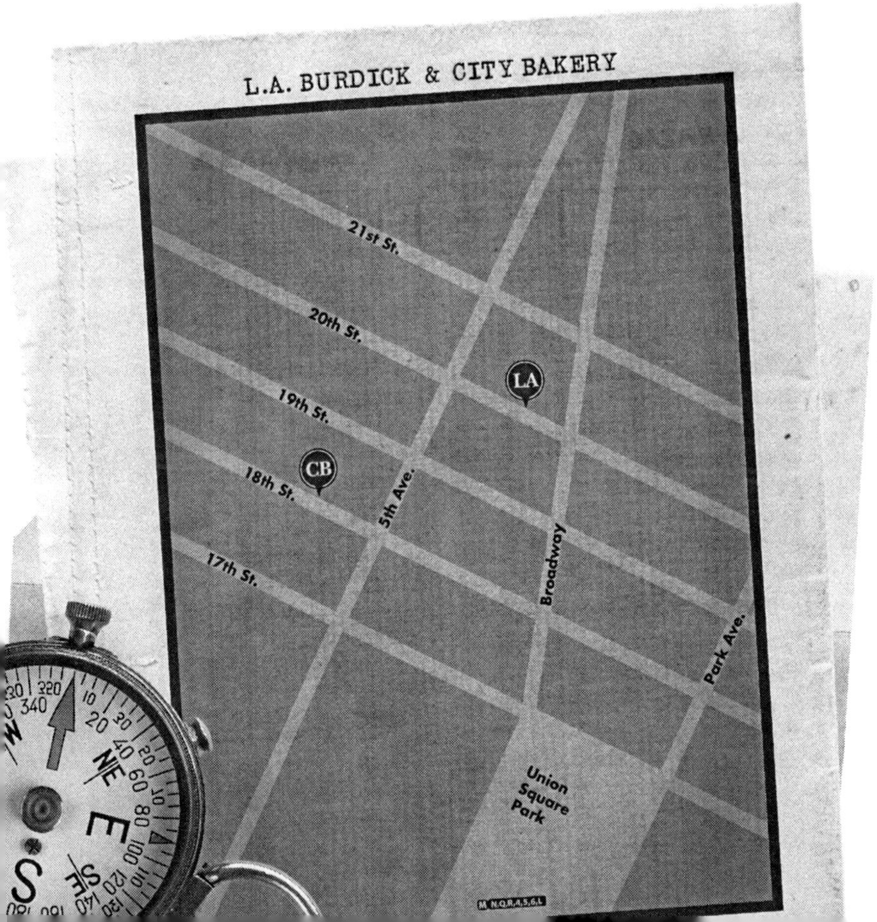

L.A. BURDICK & CITY BAKERY

Flatiron

L.A. BURDICK

5 E. 20th Street
New York, NY 10010
212.796.0143
burdickchocolate.com

MON–FRI: 7½AM – 10PM.........SAT: 8AM – 10PM...........SUN: 9AM – 9PM

🍫 CLASSIC, GRENADIAN, VENEZUELAN, DOMINICAN, BOLIVIAN, MADAGASCAN, ECUADORIAN

Move over single origin chocolate bars! For those chocolate connoisseurs who revel in your single sourced 70% Madagascar chocolate bar, well now you can quaff it. L.A. Burdick's Chocolate shop has a menu of six types of single origin hot chocolate, all lovingly detailed on their menu.

Peaking our interest, and for that matter, our taste buds as well, is the Bolivian Hot Chocolate, cultivated from wild cacao with "hints of grapefruit and tea." This is serious stuff folks, a chocolate purist's dream if you will.

Split an order into the demitasse-sized cups and sample all six. We call it the hot chocolate flight. If you plan on ordering the flight of hot chocolate, stay a while. Cozy seats and tables line the perimeter of the cottage-like shop, always festively adorned and seasonally apropos.

French pastries, and of course L.A. Burdick's famous chocolate mice (milk, dark, or white), make good friends with your palate and tummy. For best results, visit on a rainy day, the foggy windows and drink of choice will surely warm your soul.

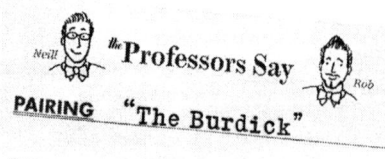

CITY BAKERY

3 W. 18th Street
New York, NY 10011
212.366.1414
thecitybakery.com

MON – FRI: 7½AM – 7PM .... SAT: 8AM – 7PM .... SUN: 10AM – 6PM

CLASSIC *(PLUS SPECIALS IN FEBRUARY...)*

Long known for their artful collection of cookies and pretzel croissants, the City Bakery also happens to be home to a decadent and extra-thick variety of hot chocolate. The signature hot chocolate is poured from vats oozing with melted chocolate goodness, seldom do we deny ourselves the pleasure of this hot chocolate concoction.

City Bakery owner, Maury Rubin, is not only the force behind City Bakery and all of its artisanal goodies, but also drives *February's Hot Chocolate Month*, now a New York City institution. Each February day brings with it a new flavor, unveiled to the masses seeking warmth and comfort. Lemon Hot Chocolate, Chili Pepper Hot Chocolate, Bourbon Hot Chocolate, and Love Potion Hot Chocolate have all been honorees. If you are at all inclined to sip a hot chocolate or two, this is an event not to be missed.

During all months of the year, City Bakery hosts a hearty happy hour, which includes mac n' cheese and beer. Pair that with some hot chocolate and Tina Fey's "I want to go to there" becomes a chorus of hungry foodies.

All guilt aside, we've been known on occasions to savor the house-made chocolate decadence in combination with a hearty repast, served buffet-style. Come meet us Tina, you know where to find us.

the Professors Say

| PAIRING | Pretzel Croissant |

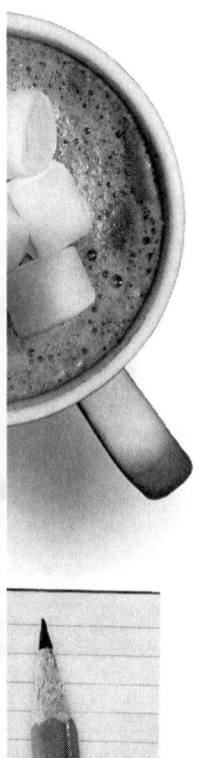

BURDICK — Iced cocoa

BURDICK —
Love (squared).

Match-Up Seven

CITY BAKERY —
To-go box

CITY BAKERY — Mallow
in the marsh!

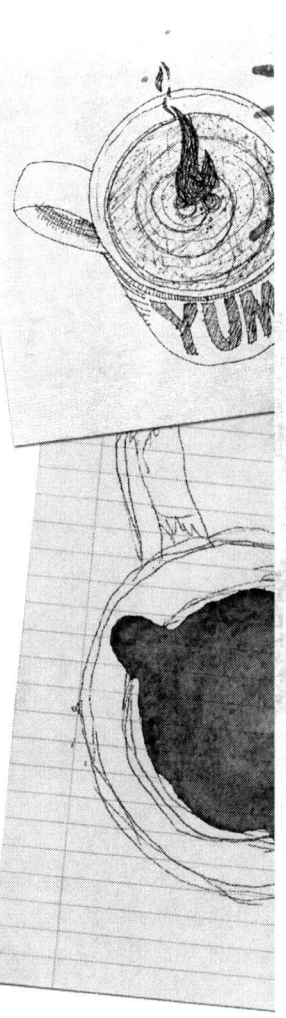

L.A. BURDICK

FLAVOR.................. ☆☆☆☆☆

TEXTURE.................. ☆☆☆☆☆

PRESENTATION......... ☆☆☆☆☆

VALUE..................... ☆☆☆☆☆

NO. 7

NAME / NOM: Flatiron

♥ Share it with us online at ♥

Match-Up Seven

CITY BAKERY

FLAVOR.................. ☆☆☆☆☆

TEXTURE................. ☆☆☆☆☆

PRESENTATION........ ☆☆☆☆☆

VALUE..................... ☆☆☆☆☆

_____
_____
_____
_____
_____
_____
_____
_____
_____
_____
_____
_____
_____

♥ www.ProfessorChocolate.com ♥

Bespoke Cocoa

RONI-SUE

Rhonda Kave [a.k.a. Roni-Sue], an entrepreneur and chocolatier, owns and operates Roni-Sue's Chocolates in the historic Essex Street Market on NYC's Lower East Side. Ever curious, Roni-Sue began exploring her most important ingredient more deeply a few years ago after visiting jungle cacao 'farms' in southern Belize. Best of all she was guided by a Mayan family who was responsible for farming and cultivating the precious cacao bean. Tasting raw rainforest grown cacao fruit right from the pod was a revelation, altering her view of chocolate forever. The daily consumption of the family's hot chocolate drink, closer in taste to cocoa tea, defined the very essence of fresh cacao.

A partnership in MOHO Chocolate Company [named for the river valley in the Toledo District of southern Belize where the cacao beans are sourced] soon followed and with ready access to fresh cocoa nibs and delicious direct trade, single origin chocolate, the hot chocolate drink experiments were on! First, using an espresso maker Roni-Sue brews a modern twist on the rich, raw chocolate flavor of the traditional Mayan beverage into a cocoa espresso. With that as a base, she adds some melted MOHO Chocolate and steamed/frothed milk for a lighter yet deeply flavorful and not too sweet hot chocolate drink. You can enjoy morning, noon & night!

Recipe No. 7

Recipe

- 3/4oz medium grind cocoa nibs
- Water for two shots espresso
- 2oz melted or shaved chocolate
- 1/2cup steamed/frothed milk

Brew the cocoa/espresso—be sure to use about half the amount of ground nibs as you would espresso to allow for expansion in the cylinder and to assure liquid flow.

Add chocolate and stir.

Top with frothed milk and some steamed milk if desired.

Match-Up Eight

Chelsea

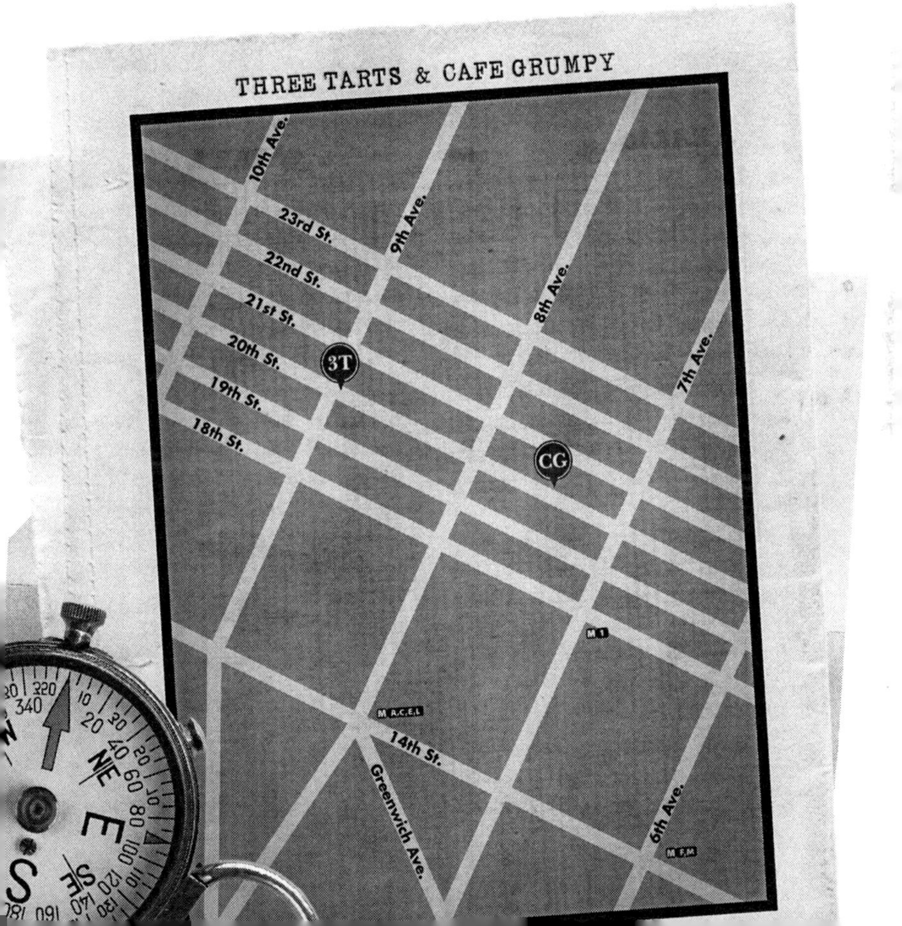

THREE TARTS & CAFE GRUMPY

Chelsea

THREE TARTS

164 9th Ave
New York, NY 10011
212.462.4392
threetarts.com

MON – SAT: 10AM – 8PM .... SUN: 11AM – 6PM

🍺 CLASSIC

If we could give an award for the most eclectic and charming chocolate boutique and gift shop, it would have to go to Three Tarts. It's named after three lovely women who went to culinary school together. Three Tarts specializes in everything ambrosial, edible and dainty. Any season is a good season to visit Three Tarts.

Summer brings the joy of handmade ice cream sandwiches and frozen hot chocolate, a favorite of the venerable Time Out New York. In fact, we amble over to Chelsea just to snarf down one of the divine ice cream sandwiches. The Three Tarts menu in cooler weather of course blends a decadent hot chocolate mix, painstakingly crafted by any one of the dedicated employees.

Peanut butter fanatics should not pass up the peanut butter hot chocolate, we certainly can't.

Six gourmet marshmallows, including cinnamon and rosemary chocolate can be added to make your hot chocolate more vivid and textured. Only the most bold and dedicated chocolate drinkers choose flavored marshmallows. Ask for advice about which marshmallow blends best with the hot chocolate, answers will certainly surprise and amuse.

Precious jewel-like pastries are honored like mini-trophies in the display case, any one makes for a delightful afternoon snack. The other half of the petite shop offers a myriad of bite-size gifts, perfect for that special someone in your life.

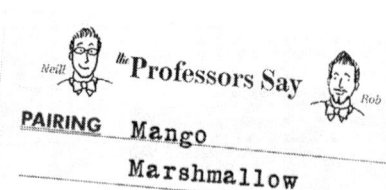

the **Professors Say**

PAIRING   Mango
          Marshmallow

Match-Up Eight

CAFE GRUMPY

224 W. 20th St
New York, NY 10011
212.255.5511
cafegrumpy.com

MON – FRI: 7AM – 8PM .... SAT: 7½AM – 8PM .... SUN: 7½AM – 7½PM

🍫 DARK PROPRIETARY BLEND

We know, we know. This book is about finding the best hot chocolate, which usually excludes the café-culture's tried and true method of mixing cocoa powder with milk and/or water.

But this is our one exception. Café Grumpy, though quite contrary to its name, exudes the utmost happiness. A smiley staff and a hot cocoa reminiscent of your childhood swiss miss, combines to make the "grumpy" experience quite convivial. Some could view their no laptop policy as a downer, we on the other hand, revel in the opportunity to converse with our friends. In fact, one could grumpily do so at their three other NYC locations- Lower East Side, Greenpoint, and of course, the over-caffeinated Park Slope.

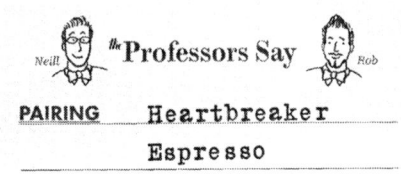

PAIRING Heartbreaker Espresso

Chelsea

3T — Buy some mix on the way out

3T — P.C. samples... repeatedly

Match-Up Eight

GRUMPY – Art of cocoa

GRUMPY – Chill vibes

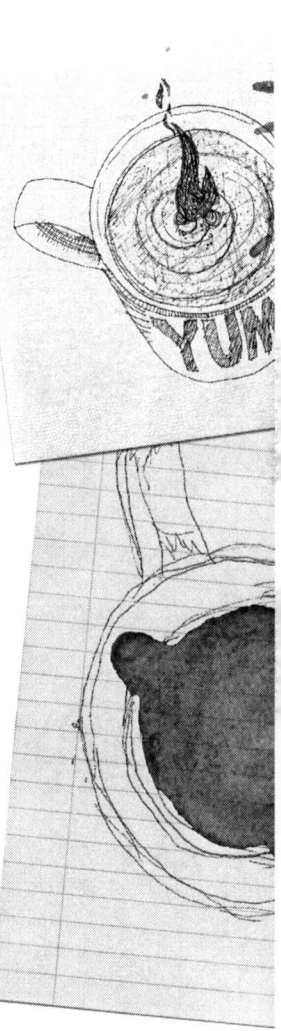

NO. 8

NAME / NOM: Chelsea

THREE TARTS

FLAVOR .... ☆☆☆☆☆

TEXTURE .... ☆☆☆☆☆

PRESENTATION .... ☆☆☆☆☆

VALUE .... ☆☆☆☆☆

♥ Share it with us online at ♥

Match-Up Eight

CAFE GRUMPY

FLAVOR............. ☆☆☆☆☆

TEXTURE............. ☆☆☆☆☆

PRESENTATION........ ☆☆☆☆☆

VALUE............... ☆☆☆☆☆

Bespoke Cocoa

PROFESSOR'S BLEND

For many years we have traipsed and snaked our way around New York City searching for only the most delectable chocolate. During this time, we have come to the conclusion that life has only a few absolutes. One of which is that we both crave, adore, and worship peanut butter. Peanut butter and chocolate you say? Bring it on. Adding to our lust of all things good, we also fell for the alluring tinge of artisanal salt. Chocolate, peanut butter, and salt—all at once, of course. Below is our own unique blend of hand-crafted ingredients that creates a rich and flavor-packed hot chocolate that will surely leave you salivating for more.

Recipe No. 8

Recipe

Salted Peanut Butter Cocoa

- 1 bar of 70 % Nói Sirius Icelandic Chocolate
- 2 heaping tbsp of Betty Lou's Organic Powdered Peanut Butter
- 2 cups of Vanilla Coconut Milk or Organic Whole Milk
- 2 large pinches of salt (we love our Fleur de Sel from The Meadow in NYC)
- 2 tbsp of organic peanut butter
- 2 tbsp of honey

In a saucepan combine the milk, powdered PB, and honey over medium heat. Add the chocolate and wait until it is completely melted. Stir continuously. Add the peanut butter, honey and salt. Stir until ingredients are well-combined and then remove from heat.

Find a mug that feels right and enjoy!!

PRIVATE CHOCOLATE TOURS

IN NEW YORK CITY, NEW YORK

WALKING TOURS:

Minimum of 4 people and maximum of 10 people for walking tours. For parties of more than 10, please inquire about one of our luxury tours...

Includes a personalized tour by Professor Chocolate, a FREE copy of *The Ultimate Guide to Finding Chocolate in NYC*, and one piece of chocolate per person per location.

TOUR OPTIONS:

- STANDARD
- LUXURY
- GLUTEN FREE
- SUGAR FREE
- DAIRY FREE
- VEGAN

(COMBINABLE)

**CONTACT:
PROFESSORCHOCOLATE
[AT]MAC.COM**

a great time for chocolate lovers!

The thing that we love to do the most (aside from eating chocolate and cheese) is to visit our favorite shops. Talking to the owners and tasting new things never gets old for us. We have developed over 25 different chocolate tours in Manhattan and Brooklyn.

— Profs.

the guidebook

PROFESSOR CHOCOLATE presents

The Ultimate Guide to Finding CHOCOLATE in NYC

LOWER MANHATTAN and BROOKLYN

ROB MONAHAN & NEILL ALLEVA

ABOUT

PROFESSOR CHOCOLATE is Rob Monahan & Neill Alleva

We are, if you are ready and so inclined, your personal tour guides through the rich vastness that is New York City chocolate. Our mission is a celebration of enthusiasm for chocolate, a call to all chocolate lovers to better love chocolate. As with all arts and aficionados, our journey is as endless as our hunger insatiable. That makes us hungry...where'd we put that chocolate?